Contents

Why Do Some Homes Move? 4

Types of Moving Homes 8

Tents Today. 14

Changing Homes 18

Moving Together 20

Around the World 22

Picture Glossary. 23

Index 24

Why Do Some Homes Move?

Some people live in homes that move.

Where We Live

Homes that Move

Heinemann
LIBRARY
Chicago, Illinois

© 2014 Heinemann Library
an imprint of Capstone Global Library, LLC
Chicago, Illinois

To contact Capstone Global Library please phone 800-747-4992, or visit our website www.capstonepub.com

All rights reserved. No part of this publication may be reproduced or transmitted in any form or by any means, electronic or mechanical, including photocopying, recording, taping, or any information storage and retrieval system, without permission in writing from the publisher.

Edited by Daniel Nunn and Abby Colich
Designed by Cynthia Akiyoshi
Picture research by Mica Brancic
Production by Sophia Argyris
Originated by Capstone Global Library

ISBN 978-1-4329-8067-2 (hc)
978-1-4329-8072-6 (pb)

Library of Congress Cataloging-in-Publication Data
Smith, Sian.
Homes that move / Sian Smith.
pages cm.—(Where we live)
Includes bibliographical references and index.
ISBN 978-1-4329-8067-2 (hb)—ISBN 978-1-4329-8072-6 (pb) 1. Dwellings—Juvenile literature. 2. Tents—Juvenile literature. 3. Mobile homes—Juvenile literature. 4. Houseboats—Juvenile literature. I. Title.
GT172.S66 2014
392.3'6—dc23 2012046428

Acknowledgments
We would like to thank the following for permission to reproduce photographs: Getty Images pp. 5 (Lonely Planet Images/Jane Sweeney); 7 (Image Source); 8 (Robert Harding World Imagery/C Gascoigne); 9 (AFP Photo/Anne-Christine Poujoulat); 10 (The Image Bank/Alan Powdrill); 14 (Lonely Planet Images/Scott Darsney); 15 (hemis.fr/Christophe Boisvieux); 17, 23 top (Panoramic Images); 18, centre top (Peter Arnold/Fred Bruemmer); 21 (Lonely Planet Images/ Doug McKinlay); Library of Congress pp. 12, 23 centre bottom (Prints & Photographs Online Catalog); Shutterstock pp. 4, 22 bottom right (© Alexandra Lande); 6 (© Galyna Andrushko); 11 (© Baloncici); 16, 22 bottom left (© Tracing Tea); SuperStock pp. 13 (National Geographic); 19, 22 top left (age fotostock/ Ton Koene); 20, 22 top right, 23 bottom (The Irish Image Collection).

Front cover photograph of a houseboat in Kerala, India, reproduced with permission of Shutterstock (© Alexandra Lande). Back cover photograph of nomads in the Kyrgyz Republic reproduced with permission of Shutterstock (© Tracing Tea).

Every effort has been made to contact copyright holders of any material reproduced in this book. Any omissions will be rectified in subsequent printings if notice is given to the publisher.

Printed in the United States 5484

Some people keep moving so their animals can find food.

Some people keep moving to sell things in different places.

Some people keep moving to see new places.

Types of Moving Homes

Some people live on houseboats.

Inside a houseboat there is a bedroom and bathroom. There is also a kitchen.

Some people live in homes on wheels.

Inside a mobile home, everything fits in a small space.

In the past, many people lived in tents.

Tents are easy to put up and take down.

Tents Today

Some people live in tents today.

Some people live in tents called chums. They move to find food for their reindeer.

Some people live in tents called yurts. Yurts can be made of wood and wool.

Some people live in tents in the desert. Tents in the desert give cover from the sun and wind.

Changing Homes

Sometimes people build a new home each time they move.

Some people live in igloos in the winter and tents in the summer.

Moving Together

Sometimes groups of people travel together.

Traveling as a group can help people stay happy and safe.

Around the World

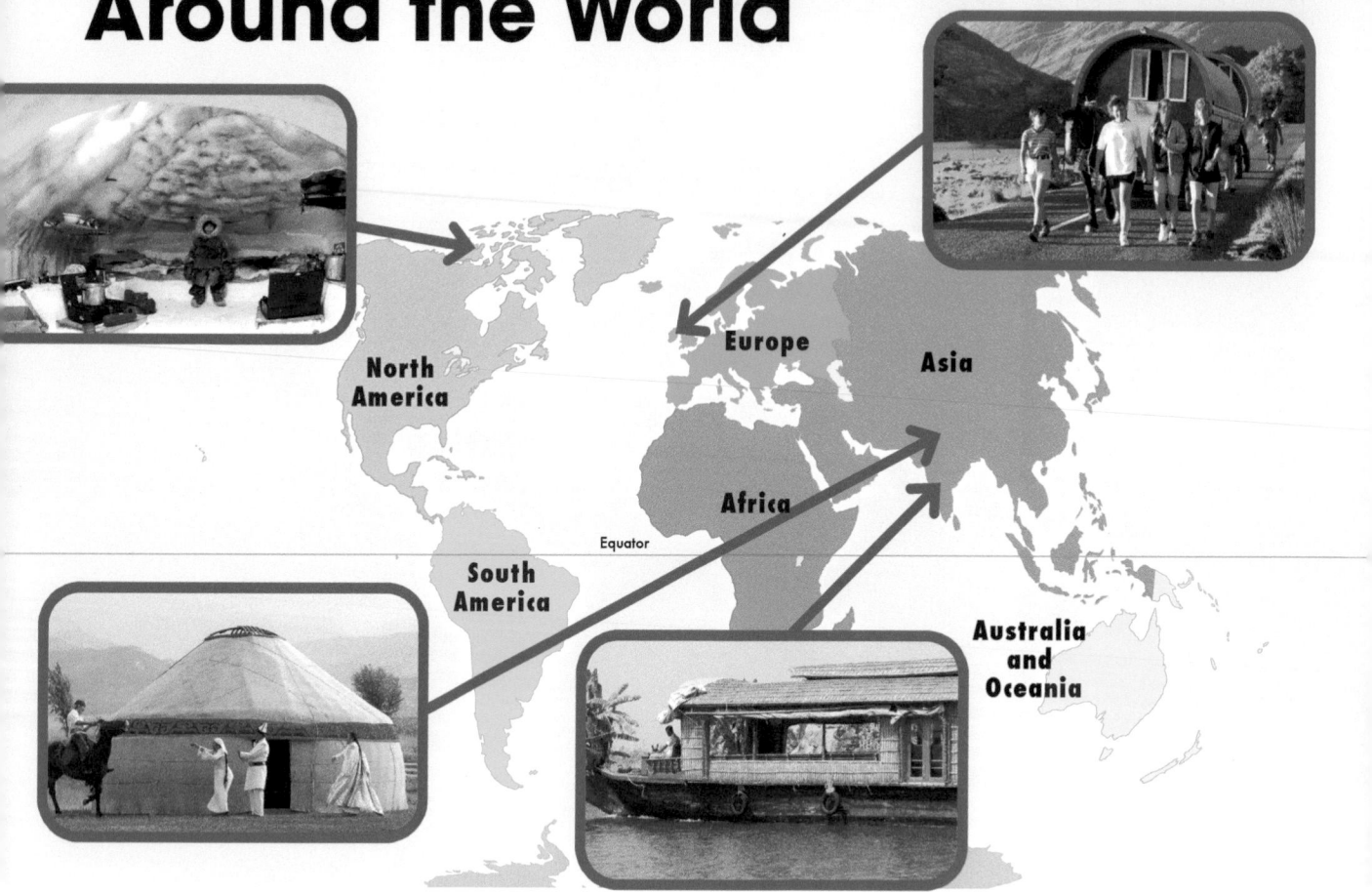

Follow the arrows to find out where each of these homes are found.

More information on page 24

Picture Glossary

desert place that does not get much rain

igloo home made from blocks of snow

tent home made from poles covered with material

travel to move around and see new places

Index

chums 15
desert 17
groups 20, 21
houseboats 8,9
igloos 18, 19
tents 12, 13, 14, 15, 16, 17, 19
yurts 16

Photograph information

The photographs in this book were taken at the following locations: p. 4 Kerala, India; p. 5 Turmi, Africa; p. 6 Daraw, Egypt; p. 7 United States; p. 8 Kashmir, India; p. 9 Marseille, France; p. 10 Florida, United States; p. 12 United States; p. 13 Russia; p. 14 Omnogov, Asia; p. 15 Khovsgol Province, Mongolia (chum is pronounced "choom"); p. 16 Kyrgyzstan; p. 17 Tunisia; p. 18 Canada; p. 19 Gojahaven, Canada; p. 20 County Mayo, Ireland; p. 21 Bamiyan, Afghanistan.

Notes for parents and teachers

Look at the title of the book and brainstorm types of moving homes the children expect to find inside. Read the book together and discuss why people might need homes that can move. Compare the insides of different homes, for example the yurt (called a "ger" in Mongolia) on page 14 and the igloo on page 19. What do the two homes have in common? Discuss how homes provide us with a place to eat and sleep, and keep people and their things safe from the weather. Use the photograph information above to select a group of people to find out more about. Help the children to research the group and discuss the importance of community, traditions, and the feelings of belonging to part of a group.